Rise & Shine!
It's Breakfast Time!

Written by
Kids Cooking Club

Illustrated by
Yancey Labat

Scholastic Inc.
New York   Toronto   London   Auckland   Sydney   Mexico City   New

No part of this publication may be reproduced in whole or in part, or stored in a retrieval system, or transmitted in any form or by any means, electronic, mechanical, photocopying, recording, or otherwise, without written permission of the publisher. For information regarding permission, write to Scholastic Inc., Attention: Permissions Department, 557 Broadway, New York, NY 10012.

Designed by Peggy Gardner

ISBN 0-439-83223-3
Copyright © 2006 by Kids Cooking Club®, La Jolla, CA. All rights reserved.
Published by Scholastic Inc.

SCHOLASTIC and associated logos are trademarks and/or registered trademarks of Scholastic Inc.

Kids Cooking Club and associated logos are trademarks and/or registered trademarks of Kids Cooking Club, LLC.

12 11 10 9 8 7 6 5 4 3   7 8 9 10/0

Printed in China

First Scholastic printing, March 2006

Good Morning!

When that first peep of sunshine peers in your window, it's time to wake up—and it's time for breakfast! Breakfast is the most important meal of the day because it provides our bodies with the fuel we need to get up and go. As an aspiring young chef, you will find out what fun it is to make breakfast! How about a morning meal of French toast sticks dipped into honey? Or how about ice cream for breakfast? Or a toad in the hole? You'll want to jump right into this great new cookbook and try all these wonderful recipes.

So rise and shine! Let's get cooking! It's a good morning, indeed!

What Every Breakfast Chef Needs to Know!

- Read the entire recipe from start to finish before you begin.
- Wash your hands with soap, wear an apron, roll up your sleeves, and pull back long hair.
- Have a clear, clean, and uncluttered work area.
- Grown up supervision is a MUST when using the stove, oven, microwave, waffle iron, vegetable peelers, cheese graters, or knives.
- Learn to clean up and put things away as you bake instead of waiting until the end.
- Keep opened items like flour, sugar, etc. in sealed plastic containers.
- Never run or play roughhouse in the kitchen.
- Keep a fire extinguisher handy in every kitchen and know how to use it.

- Have a grown-up do the following tasks for you:
  - Take bowls and containers in and out of the microwave
  - Handle hot skillets and pans
  - Turn pot handles so they face inside and won't get bumped
  - Remove lids or other covers while food is cooking
  - Use wooden spoon to stir on the stove

Note to Grown-ups:

All of the recipes in this book are designed for adult supervision at all times. Kids should never be left alone in the kitchen. There are many steps that grown-ups need to handle or supervise including, but not limited to, oven, stove, and microwave safety listed above, carrying hot pans, working with sharp knives, operating appliances, overseeing kids at the stove, and ensuring that the stove and oven are turned off after use.

We have placed this icon next to those steps that will require your help.

Important Tools Breakfast Chefs Need

Have these ready when the sun comes up, so you can get cookin':

Baking sheets: Use with biscuits, granola, and strudel.

Blender: To blend smoothies.

Breakfast drinks: Mugs, parfait glasses, fancy straws, and paper umbrellas are fun.

Round cookie cutter: Use for making biscuits.

Kids Cooking Club apron: Keeps your pj's clean.

Ladle: To spoon batter into pans.

Measuring cups & spoons: To measure wet and dry ingredients.

Mixing bowls: Use the one included in your kit. Have other sizes ready.

Mixing spoons: Use the wooden one included in your kit. Have other mixing spoons handy.

Oven mitts: Heavy mitts are best for small hands so they don't slip.

Pancake mold: Use the star shaped one in this kit to make fun shaped pancakes.

Pastry brush: Use to spread melted butter.

Pie pans: 9-inch rounds for quiche and hash brown bake.

Skillet: A must for breakfast cooking. Use a large, heavy one (cast iron is best).

Small paring knife: For coring apples, slicing and dicing fruit.

Spatula: For pancakes, eggs, and everything breakfast. Use the one in the kit.

Vegetable peeler: For peeling apples and potatoes.

Waffle iron: To cook waffles (many fun shapes are available).

Whisk: For mixing batters and whipping eggs.

Wood skewers: For fruit kebabs.

Helpful Terms & Hints

Understanding these cooking terms will help you become a great breakfast chef:

Coring: To remove the seed section from fruits. Use an apple corer or a small paring knife. Cut the apple in half and then each half in half again. Cut the core off each slice.

Crack an egg: Firmly hit the middle part of the egg on the side of a bowl. Use both hands to split open the shell and let the egg drop out. Check to remove any shell pieces.

Greased: Spray the inside of pancake mold, waffle iron, skillet, and pans with vegetable oil spray.

Granny Smith apples: Green, smooth, and firm—perfect for breakfast recipes.

Peeling: Put fruits on a cutting board and hold firmly with one hand. Peel away from yourself and keep turning the fruit as you go.

Zest: Use a large box grater to lightly rub the peel of a piece of citrus fruit (orange, lemon) off.

Perfect Pancakes

Makes about 12 pancakes

Once you master perfect pancakes, you will be a "star" in everyone's eyes!

Ingredients:

1 ½ cup all-purpose flour
3 tablespoons sugar
2 teaspoons baking powder
Pinch of salt
3 tablespoons butter, melted
1 ½ cup milk
2 eggs

Tools:

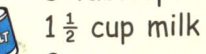

- Measuring cups & spoons
- 2 mixing bowls
- Vegetable oil spray
- Maple syrup
- Whisk
- Small microwaveable bowl
- Plastic wrap
- Skillet, greased
- Ladle
- Star shaped pancake mold, greased

STEPS:

1. Mix together flour, sugar, baking powder, and salt in one mixing bowl.

2. Melt butter in small microwaveable bowl covered with plastic wrap in microwave. Put butter in a separate mixing bowl and whisk together with milk and eggs. Add this to flour mixture and whisk until just mixed.

3. Heat greased skillet over medium heat. Lightly spray the inside of the star-shaped pancake mold with vegetable oil and place in the middle of the skillet. Carefully ladle about $\frac{1}{4}$ cup of batter into the mold and do not move or lift the mold until the pancake is set. Cook until bubbles form on the top, and the bottom is golden brown, about 4 minutes. Remove the mold, flip the pancake, and cook the other side for about 2 minutes or until lightly browned. Serve with favorite syrup or jam.

That's One Big Baked Pancake!

Not only is it gigantic, but it's also packed full of delicious goodies. Bake and slice on those mornings when you are especially starving.

Ingredients:

Perfect pancake batter from pages 9-10 or make your own batch from a box mix

3 tablespoons of sugar mixed with a pinch of cinnamon, divided

3 tablespoons of butter, melted

2 Granny Smith apples, peeled and thinly sliced

Powdered sugar and syrup for topping

Tools:

- Mixing bowl & spoon
- Measuring spoons
- Large, heavy skillet (oven proof)
- Vegetable peeler
- Small paring knife
- Toothpick

Makes 8 servings

STEPS:

1. Preheat the oven to 400°F.

2. Make the perfect pancake batter as described on pages 9-10 or per the instructions on box mix. Add 1 tablespoon of the sugar/cinnamon mixture.

3. Over low heat, melt the butter in the skillet and pour it into the pancake batter.

4. Peel and slice the apples. Arrange slices in the bottom of the frying pan. Sprinkle the remaining 2 tablespoons of sugar/cinnamon over the apples.

5. Pour the pancake batter over the sliced apples and bake (pan and all) in the oven for 20 minutes or until the center of the pancake is set and a toothpick inserted in the middle comes out clean.

6. Cool slightly and cut into pie-shaped pieces. Sprinkle top with powdered sugar and syrup and serve.

Waffles Instead?

Waffles are round and sometimes they're square. When they get cooked, they fluff up with air! If you have a waffle iron and an adult handy—these waffles are a wow!

Makes about 10 waffles

Tools:
- Measuring cups & spoons
- Waffle iron, greased
- Mixing bowl
- Whisk
- Ladle

Ingredients:
- 1½ cup all-purpose flour
- 3 tablespoons sugar
- 2 teaspoons baking powder
- Pinch of salt
- 4 tablespoons butter, melted
- 1½ cup milk
- 1 egg

Steps:
1. Heat greased waffle iron per appliance instructions.
2. Whisk together all ingredients in a mixing bowl until just blended. Pour a ladle full of batter onto iron and cook until steaming stops.

Flavor Your Waffles

Add any or all of these to your batter:

- Mini chocolate or white chips
- Chocolate sauce
- Mashed bananas
- Lemon zest
- Blueberries
- Peanut butter or butterscotch chips
- Applesauce

Top Your Waffles

For even extra sweetness, top with one of these:

- Yogurt and granola
- Whipped cream
- Powdered sugar mixed with cocoa powder
- Fresh or dried fruit
- Jam
- Chocolate or caramel sauce
- Honey

Chocolate Sauce

Ingredients:

- 8 ounces semisweet chocolate chips
- 1 cup heavy cream

Steps:

Melt chocolate in saucepan over low to medium heat. Slowly stir in cream until well blended and serve over waffles.

Crazy for Ice Cream Crêpes

Makes 10 8-inch crêpes

Ice cream for breakfast? Here is a great way to sneak it in!

Ingredients:

- 2 tablespoons butter, melted
- 2 eggs
- 1 cup milk
- 1 cup all-purpose flour
- Vanilla ice cream
- Fresh strawberries, washed and sliced
- Powdered sugar

Tools:

- Measuring cups
- Mixing bowl
- Whisk
- Skillet, greased
- Ladle
- Spatula
- Plate & foil

STEPS:

1. Whisk together melted butter, eggs, and milk in mixing bowl. Add the flour and whisk again. Then let the batter stand for 30 minutes.

2. Heat greased skillet over medium-high heat. Dip the ladle into the batter and pour batter across the pan. Cook crêpe until the batter bubbles and the sides of the crêpe lift from the pan, about 2 minutes. With a spatula, carefully lift the crêpe and flip it onto the other side. Cook for 1 minute. Put crêpe on a plate, cover with foil, and make more crêpes.

3. Place scoop of ice cream in the middle, top with sliced strawberries, and roll up crêpes. Sprinkle powdered sugar on top and eat right away.

Breakfast in Bed

Your special breakfasts are extra wonderful when you serve them to someone in bed! Here's a recipe for making the start of someone's day the best it can be!!

Unlimited Servings!

Ingredients:

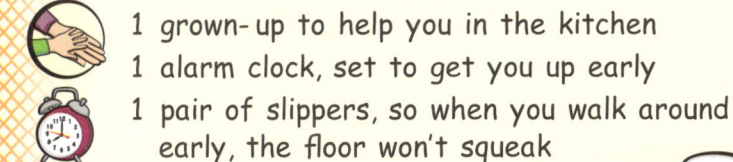

- 1 grown-up to help you in the kitchen
- 1 alarm clock, set to get you up early
- 1 pair of slippers, so when you walk around early, the floor won't squeak
- 1 breakfast tray
- 1 fresh flower in a vase
- 1 fancy plate, pretty napkin, and fine silverware
- 1 favorite breakfast (pick one from this cookbook)
- Many BIG smiles

STEPS:

1. Make a plan the night before. Tell your grown-up helper, but try to keep it a secret from the person you want to surprise.

2. Get up early and quietly make the breakfast and beverage of choice.

3. Arrange everything on the breakfast tray. Don't forget the fresh flower, maybe one from your garden.

4. Get a BIG smile ready and deliver the tray to that special someone while he or she is still in bed.

5. Make sure you let your special breakfast person know how much love went into making the breakfast. He or she will most likely share breakfast with you!!

French Toast Dipper Sticks

Serves 2-4

Making these is as fun as dipping them!

Ingredients:

- 4 slices thick French or sourdough bread
- 2 eggs
- ½ cup milk
- 1 teaspoon cinnamon
- 1 teaspoon sugar
- 2 tablespoons butter

Tools:

- Knife
- Measuring cups & spoons
- Pie pan
- Whisk
- Skillet
- Spatula
- Plate covered with foil
- Small cups

STEPS:

1. Cut each slice of bread into four even sticks.
2. Whisk together eggs, milk, cinnamon, and sugar in a pie pan.
3. Put butter into skillet over medium-high heat. Dip bread sticks into egg mixture and use your spatula to put them into the skillet. Cook several at a time until each side is golden brown. Remove dipper sticks from pan with spatula and put on a plate covered with foil. Repeat until all sticks are done.
4. Put desired dip(s) into small cups and dip away!

DIP INTO THESE:
- Maple or other flavored syrup
- Chocolate sauce
- Fresh berries pureed with sugar and orange juice
- Cheese sauce (like fondue)
- Whipped cream mixed with yogurt and jam
- Honey and cinnamon sauce
- Powdered sugar

Night-Before French Toast

This is a great plan-ahead dish for the morning. Let it soak overnight and then bake when the sun comes up!

Ingredients

12 pieces of French bread
6 eggs
1 ½ cup milk
¼ cup sugar
½ teaspoon cinnamon
1 teaspoon vanilla
2 tablespoons maple syrup
Powdered sugar, to dust top once baked

Serves 6

Tools:

- 9 x 13-inch baking pan, greased
- Measuring cups & spoons
- Whisk
- Mixing bowl
- Foil
- Spatula

STEPS:

1. Put bread slices in greased baking pan in one layer.
2. Whisk together the eggs, milk, sugar, cinnamon, vanilla, and maple syrup in a mixing bowl, then pour over the bread slices. Cover with foil and refrigerate overnight.
3. Preheat oven to 400° F.
4. Uncover and bake for 15 minutes, then have an adult turn the slices over and bake for another 5 minutes or so until browned. Lift slices onto pretty plates and dust tops with powdered sugar.

Did You Know?

French people call French toast "pain perdu," which means lost bread, because it's a way for them to use day old bread that is too dry to eat otherwise.

Get Up & Go Granola

Makes about 4 cups

Start your day out light and right!

Ingredients:

- 2 cups old fashioned oats
- 1 cup puffed cereal like Kix, Cocoa Puffs, or wheat puffs
- 1 cup toasted wheat germ
- 2 teaspoons ground cinnamon
- ¼ cup brown sugar
- ½ cup honey
- 3 tablespoons vegetable oil
- 2 teaspoons vanilla
- ½ cup raisins

Tools:

- Measuring cups & spoons
- Mixing bowls
- Large spoon
- Baking sheet with sides

Steps:

1. Preheat oven to 350°F.
2. Put oats, puffed cereal, wheat germ, cinnamon, and brown sugar into mixing bowl and stir together.
3. In another mixing bowl, mix together the honey, oil, and vanilla. Then pour this over the dry granola mixture and stir well to coat.
4. Pour mixture onto baking sheet. Bake for 20-25 minutes and have an adult stir it every 5 to 10 minutes until it is crisp and golden brown. Remove from oven and let cool. Stir in raisins.

How to Enjoy Granola

- ❖ Eat with milk
- ❖ Serve with sliced bananas, strawberries, and apples
- ❖ Layer with yogurt and sliced fruit to make a parfait
- ❖ Sprinkle as topping on yogurt
- ❖ Put in plastic bag and tie up with pretty ribbon to give to a friend
- ❖ Sprinkle in perfect pancake batter to make delicious granola pancakes

Funky Monkey Chunky Chocolate Porridge

Serves 2

Here's a simple, sweet way to start the day.

Ingredients:

- 2 packets of instant oatmeal
- 1 1/3 cup milk plus 1/4 cup more for over cereal
- 2 teaspoons maple syrup
- 1 tablespoon brown sugar
- 1/2 banana, peeled and sliced
- 2 tablespoons mini chocolate chips

Tools:

- Microwaveable bowl
- Measuring cups & spoons
- Large spoon
- 2 serving bowls

Steps:

1. Put oatmeal packets in microwaveable bowl.
2. Add the 1 1/3 cup of milk and microwave for 2 minutes and then stir in cereal.
3. Stir in maple syrup and brown sugar.
4. Divide oatmeal into two serving bowls and pour the remaining 1/4 cup of milk evenly over each bowl. Garnish with banana slices and chocolate chips.
5. You could also make a face in your bowl by using the bananas for the eyes and nose and the chocolate chips to create a big, happy smile.

Read on for more ideas for creating smiley face cereal bowls.

Smiley Face Cereal Bowls

Brighten up your day with a smiley face—in your cereal bowl! Top your daily cereal with one of these happy face ideas or try your own.

For Faces

- Half of canned peach or pear, drained
- Orange sections
- Sliced cantaloupe, honeydew
- Grapes
- Pineapple, apple, banana slices
- Fruit rolls cut into shapes

Eyes/Ears/Nose/Mouth

- Cheerios, fruit loops, or other flavored cereal
- Strawberry
- Raisins or other dried fruit pieces
- Maraschino cherries
- Mini marshmallows

Hair

- Dried apple chips
- Brown sugar chunks

Blueberry Mug O' Muffins

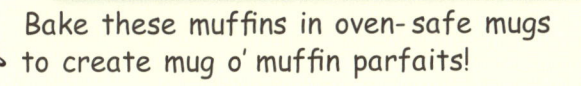

Makes 6 Mug O' Muffins

Bake these muffins in oven-safe mugs to create mug o' muffin parfaits!

Ingredients:

- 2 cups flour
- 1 tablespoon baking powder
- ¾ cup sugar
- ½ teaspoon salt
- 1 egg
- 1 cup milk
- ¼ cup vegetable oil
- 1 cup fresh blueberries (plus extra for topping)
- Whipped cream

Tools:

- Mixing bowls & spoon
- Measuring cups & spoons
- Six 8-ounce ovenproof, microwave and dishwasher safe mugs, lightly greased
- Toothpick

STEPS:

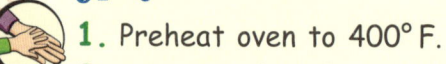

1. Preheat oven to 400° F.
2. Stir together flour, baking powder, sugar, and salt in mixing bowl.
3. In another mixing bowl, add egg, milk, and oil and mix well. Pour egg mixture into dry ingredients. Add most of the blueberries and mix until ingredients are just combined.
4. Fill each mug to ½ full with batter. Bake for 25-35 minutes or until toothpick inserted in middle comes out clean. Let mugs cool completely before topping.
5. Top with whipped cream and fresh blueberries for a mug o' muffin parfait!

Orangey, Nutty Breakfast Biscuits

These tangy and tasty biscuits are best when served warm from the oven with honey!

Ingredients:

- 1 orange
- 2 cups flour plus a little extra for dusting
- ½ teaspoon salt
- 1 tablespoon unsalted butter
- 1 cup pecan pieces
- Honey

Tools:

- Grater
- Measuring cups & spoons
- Mixing bowl
- 2 butter knives
- Rolling pin
- Round cookie cutter
- Baking sheet, greased

Serves 6

Steps:

1. Preheat oven to 425°F.
2. Make orange zest by carefully grating the outside peel of the orange. Then cut orange and squeeze the juice into a large measuring cup. Add water until you have $1\frac{1}{2}$ cups of liquid.
3. Put flour and salt into mixing bowl. Cut in the butter with the 2 butter knives until mixture resembles coarse crumbs. Add grated orange zest and orange juice mixture and mix together until dough forms a ball.
4. Put dough on a lightly floured surface and knead in pecan pieces.
5. Dust rolling pin and roll out dough to $\frac{1}{4}$ to $\frac{1}{2}$-inch thick. Cut out biscuits using a round cookie cutter.
6. Place on greased baking sheet. Bake for about 20 minutes or until golden brown. Serve warm with honey.

Doughnut Cake

Celebrate a birthday by making a cake out of doughnuts! Actually, you can make this any time of day because it's quite fun and very colorful.

How to Make A Doughnut Cake

- ❖ You will need 2 dozen assorted doughnuts. Make sure you pick out all shapes (bars, twists, buns, regular round cake, crullers and fritters) and different flavors (cream filled, powdered, all-flavored iced, topped with colorful sprinkles, nuts, cinnamon-sugar, and glazed). The more variations, the better.

- ❖ A large sturdy serving platter

- ❖ Candles

Building the cake:

Building the cake is similar to using Lincoln logs. You want to place the larger, sturdier doughnuts on the bottom and build up as many layers as you can. Secure the doughnuts by piecing them together like a puzzle using different sizes and types that fit well together; the icing and glaze on the tops of some will help hold them in place. Save the most colorful one for the top. Put candles on the different layers and sing away! The best part is that you don't need to cut the cake. Everyone can just grab a doughnut!

bottom layer

second layer

third layer

fourth layer

34

Toast of the Town

Next time you think about having plain toast, try one of these delicious spreads!

Strawberry Cream Cheese

1/4 cup fresh ripe strawberries
1-2 teaspoons of sugar, to taste
4 ounces of cream cheese

Try blueberries, blackberries, or boysenberries for variation!

Steps:

1. Mash the strawberries in a small bowl with a fork to "puree" and add the sugar.
2. Break up the cream cheese into small pieces. Mash together with the pureed strawberries until they form a yummy, pink spread.
3. Pack the spread into a small serving dish. Cover with plastic wrap and chill until served.

Tools:

- Mixing bowl & fork
- Measuring cups & spoons
- Small serving dish
- Plastic wrap

Citrus Butter

1 lemon & 1 orange, washed
1½ sticks unsalted butter, room temperature

Steps:

1. Use the finest side of a grater to zest the lemon and orange peel into a small bowl.

2. Cut orange in half. Squeeze the orange juice into another bowl and remove the seeds. Put the butter and orange and lemon zest into a blender and blend quickly. Add the orange juice and blend again until mixed. Scrape the butter into a small serving dish. Cover with plastic wrap and chill until served.

Tools:
- Grater
- Mixing bowls
- Knife
- Blender
- Small serving dish
- Plastic wrap

Heavenly Hash Brown Pie

Serves 6

Please do try our hash brown pie. It's delicious, that is why!

Ingredients:

- 3 cups shredded hash brown potatoes
- 1/3 cup butter, melted
- 6 slices pre-cooked bacon, crumbled
- 3 stalks green onions, sliced
- 1 cup grated cheddar cheese
- 2 eggs
- 1/2 cup milk
- 1/2 teaspoon salt
- 1/4 teaspoon black pepper
- Sour cream for top

Tools:

- 9-inch pie pan
- Small microwaveable bowl
- 2 mixing bowls
- Knife
- Cutting board
- Grater
- Whisk

1. Preheat oven to 425°F.
2. Press hash browns onto the bottom and sides of a 9-inch pie pan.
3. Melt butter in a small microwaveable bowl. Drizzle melted butter over hash browns. Bake for 20 minutes or until just light brown.
4. Crumble up bacon into pieces and put them in a mixing bowl. Add green onions. Add grated cheese.
5. In another bowl, whisk together eggs, milk, salt, and pepper.
6. Spread bacon, onion, and cheese mixture over baked hash browns. Then pour in egg mixture.
7. Reduce oven temperature to 350°F. Bake for 25 minutes or until golden. Let cool for at least 5 minutes before slicing and serving. Dollop slices with sour cream.

How Would You Like Your Eggs?

There are many ways to prepare eggs. Learn these terms and experiment!

Fried over-easy:
cooked whole out of shell with the second side cooked lightly so still runny.

Fried over-hard:
cooked whole out of shell with both sides cooked well.

Hard-boiled:
cooked in shell in very hot water until white and yolk are both solid, then peeled.

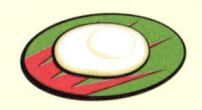

Poached:
cooked whole out of the shell in simmering water or another liquid.

Soft-boiled:
cooked in shell in very hot water until white is set and yolk is soft, then peeled open to eat with a spoon.

Sunny-side up:
cooked whole out of shell with the only bottom side cooked.

Scrambled:
whisked together with milk and cooked in a pan into firm small pieces.

Crack Me Up Jokes

What do you call an egg that cracks a good joke?

Practical yolker

What do you call a bird that's afraid of its shadow?

A chicken

Why do chickens lay eggs?

So they don't break!

What do you call a city made of eggs?

New Yolk City

Easy, Not Hard Boiled Eggs

Over easy...you betcha and easy to make, too! Serve these with Orangey, Nutty Breakfast Biscuits on pages 31-32.

INGREDIENTS:

4 eggs
About 8 cups water
About 6 cups iced water

TOOLS:
- Saucepan
- Measuring cup
- Medium bowl
- Slotted spoon

MAKES 4 EGGS

STEPS:

1. Lay eggs in saucepan and cover with water by about 2 inches. Bring to a boil and cook for 2 minutes.

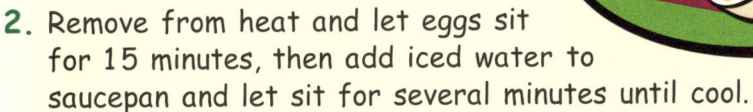

2. Remove from heat and let eggs sit for 15 minutes, then add iced water to saucepan and let sit for several minutes until cool.

3. Peel and eat.

Toad in the Hole

Can you guess what this is? It's an egg of course, fried in the middle of a slice of bread. When it is cooked, the toad peeps out of its hole at you.

Tools:
- Glass
- Knife
- Spatula
- Skillet

Ingredients:
1 slice of bread
1 egg
butter

Steps:

1. Take a slice of bread (thicker is better) and cut a hole in the middle using a glass as a cookie cutter. Butter each side of the remaining slice.
2. Fry the buttered bread in a skillet like grilled cheese.
3. After you flip it over to grill the second side, break an egg in the hole to fry.
4. Cook until egg is well done and serve!

Have an Omelet Party

Makes 1 omelet per person

Have a party at breakfast! Invite your friends over and have them each bring a goody for the omelets. Use some of our ideas or come up with your own!

Ingredients for You to Provide:

- 2 eggs (per omelet)
- Butter
- 1 tablespoon water
- Salt
- Pepper

Ingredients for Your Guests to Bring:

- Crumbled bacon
- Diced sausage
- Diced tomatoes
- Chopped bell peppers - all colors
- Chopped green onions
- Chopped onion
- Sliced spinach or mushrooms
- Favorite cheese grated
- Potatoes, cooked and cubed
- Shrimp or crab (fancy!)

Make copies of the "Eggy Word Scramble" on page 55 and let your guests try to unscramble the words.

Tools:

- Assortment of small bowls
- Measuring spoons
- Skillet, greased
- Spatula
- Baking sheet covered with foil

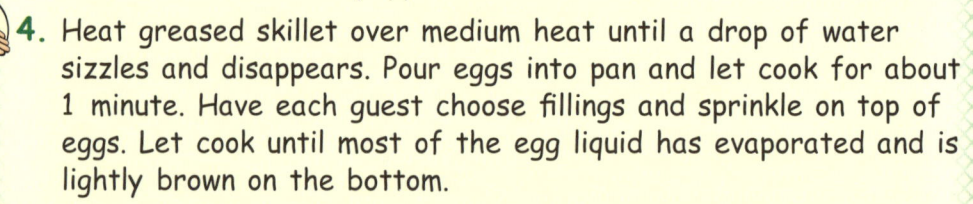

1. Turn oven on warm.
2. Put guests' ingredients into assorted small bowls and set up an area near (but not on) the stove where your friends can select which items they want to include in their omelets.
3. In another small bowl, crack 2 eggs and beat with 1 tablespoon of water per omelet. Add salt and pepper to taste.
4. Heat greased skillet over medium heat until a drop of water sizzles and disappears. Pour eggs into pan and let cook for about 1 minute. Have each guest choose fillings and sprinkle on top of eggs. Let cook until most of the egg liquid has evaporated and is lightly brown on the bottom.
5. Carefully fold the omelet in half with a spatula and slide onto a baking pan covered with foil. Keep warm in oven while you repeat this process with your other guests, so you can all eat at once.

Nick's Breakfast Burrito

MAKES 4 SERVINGS

A very special boy makes these very special egg burritos every Sunday morning. Try them once and you'll see why they are a family favorite.

Ingredients:

- 8 eggs
- ¼ cup milk
- ½ cup red bell pepper, diced
- ½ cup green onion, sliced
- 6 slices Canadian bacon, diced
- ½ cup sharp cheddar cheese, grated
- Salt and pepper
- 8 flour tortillas
- Salsa

Guacamole

Peel and mash 2 ripe avocados in a small bowl. Squeeze fresh lime juice in and add 1 small clove of garlic, minced. Add salt and pepper to taste and 1 spoonful of salsa.

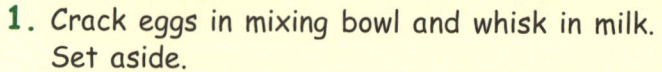

1. Crack eggs in mixing bowl and whisk in milk. Set aside.

2. On a cutting board, dice and slice the red bell pepper, green onion, and Canadian bacon. Add these items to egg mixture and whisk together. Add grated cheese and salt and pepper to taste.

3. Heat a skillet over medium heat. Add egg mixture and cook, stirring regularly until eggs are firmly scrambled. Turn off heat.

4. Heat the flat frying pan over low-medium heat. Put in flour tortillas one at a time and lightly brown the bottoms for about 1 minute, then turn over and lightly brown other side. Put on serving plate covered with foil to keep warm while you cook all the tortillas.

5. Place a scoop of cooked egg mixture in the middle of each tortilla. Add guacamole and salsa to taste and fold up like a burrito. Muy Bueno!

Tools:
- Mixing bowl
- Measuring cups
- Whisk
- Knife
- Cutting board
- Skillet, lightly greased
- Spatula
- Flat frying pan
- Serving plate with foil

Real Kids Do Eat Quiche!

SERVES 6

Quiche is not just for breakfast. It makes a nice brunch, lunch, dinner, or evening snack.

INGREDIENTS:

9-inch pre-made pie crust, found at grocery store

2 cups Swiss cheese, grated

½ cup Canadian bacon or ham, diced

5 eggs

1 ¼ cup milk

Pinch of ground black pepper

Pinch of nutmeg

TOOLS:

- 9-inch pie or quiche pan, lightly greased
- Grater
- Large mixing bowl
- Whisk
- Toothpick

STEPS:

1. Preheat oven to 375°F.
2. Line quiche or pie pan with pie dough.
3. Grate cheese and put in pie shell.
4. Crack eggs into mixing bowl and beat lightly with whisk. Add milk, pepper, nutmeg, and diced bacon or ham, and mix. Then pour over cheese.
5. Bake for 40 minutes or until a toothpick inserted in the center comes out clean.

Cool for at least 5 minutes before slicing and eating.

WHEN TO SERVE QUICHE?

Serve quiche on Mother's Day,

Serve quiche in a fancy way,

Serve quiche to impress Grandpa,

Serve quiche when you crave something eggstra!

Krazy Fruit Kebabs

Makes lots of skewers

These colorful kebabs are a refreshing treat to serve with any breakfast dish!

Ingredients:
- 1 cup fresh pineapple, chunked
- 1 cup strawberries, thickly sliced
- 1 cup seedless grapes, stems taken off
- 1 cup melon of choice, chunked
- 1 cup raspberries
- 1 cup bananas, thickly sliced

Tools:
- Cutting board
- Knife
- Measuring cup
- Wooden skewers
- Fancy serving platter

Steps:
1. Wash and dry all fruit (except bananas) then prepare as noted above.
2. Carefully slide fruit pieces onto skewers, alternating one fruit at a time. Arrange on nice beautiful serving platter.

Tutti-Frutti Parfaits

Serves 4

The sweet layers make parfaits taste and look so good!

Ingredients:

- 1 cup fresh strawberries, sliced
- 1 pint fresh blackberries, raspberries, or blueberries
- 3 cups vanilla nonfat yogurt
- 1 cup granola
- Whipped cream

Tools:

- Measuring cups
- Large spoon
- 4 parfait glasses or large wine glasses

Steps:

1. Wash and prepare fruit. Combine strawberries with fresh berries of choice.
2. Layer parfaits into 4 glasses as follows: start with $\frac{1}{3}$ cup vanilla yogurt in the bottom and alternate layers of fruit, granola and yogurt until glasses are full. Top each with whipped cream.

Sunshine Smoothies

ALL RECIPES ARE FOR 2 SERVINGS

DRINK THESE IN FUN SHAPED GLASSES WITH A LONG CRAZY STRAW AND PAPER UMBRELLAS!

Berry Banana Smoothie

1 small banana, peeled and sliced

¼ cup fresh or frozen berries (such as raspberries, blueberries, blackberries and/or strawberries)

1 cup orange juice

3 tablespoons vanilla yogurt

Peanut Butter Smoothie

2 cups vanilla or chocolate ice cream

½ cup milk

3 tablespoons peanut butter

Pineapple Strawberry Smoothie

1 cup fresh pineapple chunks

1 cup frozen strawberries

1 cup vanilla yogurt

¾ cup milk

Blend all ingredients for each smoothie in blender until smooth

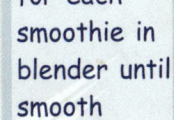

Chocolate Banana Smoothie

2 small bananas, peeled and sliced 
1 $\frac{1}{2}$ cup milk
1 cup chocolate pudding
$\frac{1}{4}$ teaspoon cinnamon

Black Forest Smoothie

2 cups chocolate ice cream 
1 $\frac{1}{2}$ cup milk
3 tablespoons cherry pie filling

Tropical Smoothie

1 cup vanilla yogurt 
1 $\frac{1}{2}$ cup milk
$\frac{1}{2}$ cup crushed pineapple

Hot Morning Sippers

SERVES 1

These flavor-your-own hot drinks will warm your soul first thing in the morning!

Flavor Your Own Hot Cocoa

Start With:
2 teaspoons sugar
1 teaspoon cocoa powder
1 cup cold milk

Optional Additions:
¼ teaspoon mint
¼ teaspoon vanilla
1 teaspoon raspberry jam

Topping Choices:
Whipped cream
Shaved chocolate
Chocolate jimmies
Mini marshmallows

What to do:
In saucepan, stir together sugar, cocoa powder, milk, and any optional additions. Bring to just before a boil. Pour into mug and top with toppings!

Flavor Your Own Spiced Apple Cider

Start With:
1 cup apple cider
1 cinnamon stick
Pinch of ground nutmeg

Optional Additions:
½ cup apple cider and ½ cup cranberry juice
Sprinkle of cinnamon and nutmeg instead of cinnamon stick
Add a slice of orange
Sprinkle in a few dried cranberries or fresh raspberries
Add a couple slices of apples

Topping Choices:
Whipped cream
Lemon slices
Orange wedges
Brown sugar sprinkles

What to do:
Put apple cider, cinnamon stick, pinch of ground nutmeg, and any optional additions in a saucepan. Heat over medium-high heat until steam rises. Pour into mug and top with toppings!

Serves 1

Unscramble These Eggs!

Answers on page 56

1. epkaacn _____
(Hint: It's flat but you made it into a star)

2. ktebarsfani dbe _____
(Hint: A morning treat)

3. naoalrg _____
(Hint: A type of cereal)

4. hhsa nwbor _____
(Hint: Made from potatoes)

5. leeomt _____
(Hint: Made with eggs)

6. felfwa _____
(Hint: Sometimes square sometimes round)

It Was a Good Morning, Indeed!

Every morning when you make and eat something delicious and good for you, is a great way to start any day. That first meal can set the tone for the whole day and provide the boost you need to do well in school, shine in sports, and carry you through until midday. And speaking of lunch, guess what's coming next...a fabulous new cookbook all about the lunch and great things to eat in the middle of the day! So now that you have mastered breakfast, you can look forward to more good cooking with Kids Cooking Club!

Every great chef takes good care of his or her kitchen and tools, so remember to clean up after you cook and take good care of the cooking gifts in this package by hand washing and drying them after each use.

See you next time and don't forget that preparing Breakfast-In-Bed for someone is a great way to show you care!

❖

Check out www.kidscook.com for more delicious fun for everyone!

Answers from page 55: 1. pancake 2. breakfast in bed 3. granola 4. hash brown 5. omelet 6. waffle